LET'S PLAY TWO

I0139516

Anthony Clarvoe

BROADWAY PLAY PUBLISHING INC
New York
www.broadwayplaypublishing.com
info@broadwayplaypublishing.com

Cover photo by Henry DiRocco, usage by arrangement with South Coast Repertory

LET'S PLAY TWO was first published in the collection *Plays By Anthony Clarvoe* in January 1996

First printing of this edition: August 2020
I S B N: 978-0-88145-876-3

Book design: Marie Donovan
Page make-up: Adobe Indesign
Typeface: Palatino

LET'S PLAY TWO was commissioned by South Coast Repertory. It was presented in South Coast Repertory's NewSCRipts series as a workshop directed by Barton DeLorenzo, and by the Playwrights' Center as a workshop directed by Kent Stephens.

The world premiere of LET'S PLAY TWO was presented on 22 September 1992 by South Coast Repertory (David Emmes, Producing Artistic Director; Martin Benson, Artistic Director). The cast and creative contributors were:

PHIL ....Arye Gross
GRACE... Susan Cash

Director.. Michael Bloom
Set ....John Iacovelli
Lighting... Brian Gale
Costumes..Dwight Richard Odle
Music & sound ....Nathan Birnbaum
Stage manager..Andy Tighe

ACKNOWLEDGMENTS

In addition to the above, my thanks also go to Jerry Patch, John Glore, Lisa Wasserman, and Robin Goodrin Nordli at South Coast Repertory, and to David Moore, Jeffrey Hatcher, J C Cutler, and Sally Wingert at the Playwrights' Center for their help in shaping the play.

I thank the John Simon Guggenheim Foundation, the McKnight Foundation, and the Playwrights' Center for their generous financial support during the writing of LET'S PLAY TWO.

CHARACTERS & SETTING

GRACE, *age 34*
PHIL, *age 27*

Time and place: Minnesota and elsewhere. Baseball season, 1991.

Set: Something suggesting a car. A piece of open road that rapidly becomes several different rooms defined by a single piece of furniture. Enough space to dance in.

I see great things in baseball. It's our game—the American game. It will take our people out-of-doors, fill them with oxygen, give them a larger physical stoicism. Tend to relieve us from being a nervous, dyspeptic set. Repair these losses, and be a blessing to us.
Walt Whitman

It's a great day for a ballgame. Let's play two!
Ernie Banks

ACT ONE

Scene One

(A horn honks. Lights up on PHIL *sitting in the car, wearing a serviceable dark blue suit. The engine is running. His door is open, he's leaning out and looking up.)*

PHIL: Grace? *(He honks the horn again.)* Grace! We're running late!

GRACE: *(Off)* Coming!

PHIL: You want me to come up?

GRACE: Down in a sec!

*(*PHIL *shuts the door and turns on the radio. He flips through the static along the dial until he finds a song he likes. The rhythm is a deep pounding and a higher, faster sound. The vocals are sampled and scratched and hard to make out.)*

(He turns up the volume and taps the steering wheel.)

*(*GRACE *runs in, wearing an overcoat over a large dress we can't see. She opens the passenger door, slides in, and slams the door.)*

GRACE: Drive like hell.

*(*GRACE *and* PHIL *kiss. While they do, he feels for the radio and turns it to an oldies station.)*

GRACE: Thank you.

(The kiss goes on.)

PHIL: Aren't you hot in that?

GRACE: Don't start.

PHIL: Why not?

GRACE: We're gonna be late. You know what happens.

PHIL: I like what happens.

(GRACE *pulls away.*)

GRACE: Drive. The car.

PHIL: I'll drive the car.

(PHIL *pulls into traffic. They get themselves straightened out.*)

GRACE: Good morning.

PHIL: Good morning. Did they give you a map?

GRACE: I've got directions.

PHIL: They didn't put in one of those little slips of paper with the cartoon map on it? What kind of wedding invitation is that?

GRACE: Julia—that's the bride—

PHIL: Julia—bride. The bride's name is Julia. Okay. I've gotta get all this before we get there.

GRACE: You'll have plenty of time. Why does being a bride give you permission to go insane? It hadn't really sunk in— Look at these directions. They're two pages long. Do you have a map?

PHIL: Sure, somewhere.

GRACE: Of the entire Midwest? She said she wanted the ceremony by a lake, I thought no problem, it's Minnesota—

PHIL: Ten thousand lakes, plenty to go around.

GRACE: I think she picked Lake Tanganyika.

PHIL: Source of the Nile? Excellent choice. I'll need to stop for gas.

GRACE: Sorry about this.

PHIL: Believe me, I love a long drive.

GRACE: Do you think anyone saw what I'm wearing under this?

PHIL: I can't even see it.

GRACE: Good.

PHIL: What does it look like?

GRACE: It's a bridesmaid's dress. It looks like a Halloween costume. Wave to the Metrodome.

PHIL: Hello, Dome!

GRACE: World's biggest diaphragm.

PHIL: Goodbye, Dome!

GRACE: Wish you were here!

PHIL: That's what we should do, blow this off and go to a game.

GRACE: They're playing in Kansas City.

PHIL: I know. Talkin' 'bout a road trip. *(Singing)* Oh, I'm going to Kansas City, Kansas City here I come— everybody! —They've got some overpaid relief pitchers there—

GRACE: *(Singing)* And I'm gonna get me one.

PHIL: All right! A bow bow bow bow...

GRACE: I appreciate you going to this with me. You're very brave.

PHIL: It's nothing.

GRACE: You're the first man I've known who'd be my date at a wedding.

PHIL: Why?

GRACE: God, you're young.

PHIL: Shut up. What's wrong with weddings? It's
a one-, maybe two-stop date. All the usual dating
questions, poof! Gone! "Geez, what'll I wear?" Blue
suit, no problem. "Entertainment?" The ceremony! I
laughed, I cried. "Where do we eat?" End of the hall,
sir, Ballroom Number Two. "Do we go for drinks?"
Champagne punch, there you go. "Dancing?" Sleazy
little cover band, at your service. And the killer: "Will
she wind up in a romantic mood?" Well, I think we
both know the answer to that one.

GRACE: And I even paid for the gift.

PHIL: I'm telling you, it's great. Come on, you love
weddings.

GRACE: Love weddings? No.

PHIL: Then why do you go to so many?

GRACE: I get invited. Somebody you care for goes
through something big, it's your duty to be there for
them.

PHIL: You make it sound like chemotherapy. That can't
be why.

GRACE: Look, it's different from your idea of a good
time.

PHIL: Tell me.

GRACE: I stare at the bride. She's standing there, and
you forget that she made you buy a two hundred-
dollar red taffeta ball gown for a daytime lakeshore
wedding. She's wearing that long white dress, it's
as bright as a movie screen, you stare at it, and your
eyes.... It's weird.

PHIL: What?

GRACE: I start watching movies on her. All the times
I've known her. We're all standing there, her family

and the groom and the priest, And I'm watching the
bride crawl all over some frat boy you can bet she
never mentioned to any of them. Then I see her in the
snow pushing a hatchback full of everything I own.
Now she's practically shoving me at her brother,
who back in real life is ten feet away in a bad tuxedo.
Now she's laughing till snot comes out of her nose.
Now she's introducing a guy. She's got this bright
animal look that says, "Please just tell me he's perfect."
And now she's standing next to the guy. Wearing
a wedding gown. And soon I'm gonna watch her
go away. So you cry a little. And that's what I do at
weddings. You asked.

PHIL: You're a way more serious person than I am.

GRACE: I'm sorry.

PHIL: No! I learn a lot. I've never done that.

GRACE: What do you do at a wedding?

PHIL: Point at the groom and laugh. Were you doing
that at Bob and Cindy's wedding?

GRACE: Yes, and I was doing that at Kyle and
Suzannah's wedding.

PHIL: Here we go—

GRACE: Where we met.

PHIL: We met at Bob and Cindy's wedding.

GRACE: We met at Kyle and Suzannah's—I asked
you and some other guy to move a couch out of the
dressing room. I can't believe you don't remember
something from eight weeks ago.

PHIL: I'm supposed to remember that? Some lady in a
big dress asks me to move a couch?

GRACE: Yes, you are supposed to remember that.
"Some lady?" (*She takes a compact from her purse and
looks at herself.*)

PHIL: You okay?

GRACE: Do I look like I'm not okay?

PHIL: You look great.

GRACE: I look green. God, who does your makeup, Earl Scheib?

PHIL: Hey. I got to *know* you at Bob and Cindy's wedding. Six weeks ago. And then of course we mmhmhmhmhm after Kurt and Shelley's wedding. Five weeks ago. See, I remember this stuff. Hey, let me ask you—this thing where you look at the bride. Do you do this a lot?

GRACE: Only with people I care for.

PHIL: Huh. You just look at her—

(GRACE *leaves the car and enters a different light, with talk and laughter and music in the background.*)

PHIL: And you see her doing things from before?

(PHIL *crosses toward* GRACE, *who is sitting and staring. She wears a far-too-elaborate bridesmaid's gown. The sounds of a baseball broadcast, audible but indistinct.*)

GRACE: Come on, come on...

PHIL: Hello?

GRACE: Sorry?

PHIL: Are the, uh—

GRACE: Hi.

PHIL: Do you know where they've put the coats?

GRACE: No.

PHIL: Oh. Sorry, hi. I'm Phil. Some wedding, huh?

GRACE: Some kind of wedding. Grace, yeah, nice to see you again.

PHIL: Doesn't Cindy look great?

GRACE: Especially compared to what she made the bridesmaids wear.

PHIL: Really, no, you look—

GRACE: *(Reacting to something she sees)* Oh, Jesus!

PHIL: You okay?

GRACE: Fine. Thanks.

PHIL: You sure?

GRACE: Yeah. Little spasm, there.

PHIL: Are you having, uh—should I tell anyone...?

GRACE: No, no—

PHIL: Get you anything?

GRACE: No.

PHIL: Is the T V bothering you?

GRACE: No! Uh, that's okay...

PHIL: Hey! That's the Twins game!

GRACE: Oh, yeah, so it is. I'm okay, I'll come back in a minute.

PHIL: He's bunting! Come on, he's gonna—beats it out, damn—

GRACE: Shit, Aguilera, field your position! *(Pause)* It happened to be on, so I've been, uh... *(Pause)* Cindy thinks I have cramps, don't tell, okay?

PHIL: Sure. What's the score?

GRACE: Three to two Minnesota, bottom of the ninth, one away. Did she throw the bouquet yet?

PHIL: Yeah.

GRACE: Who caught it?

PHIL: Cathy.

GRACE: Cathy who?

PHIL: Cathy my date.

GRACE: Uh-huh. And you're in here because...?

PHIL: I was looking for the coats.

GRACE: Sure.

PHIL: No, really—

GRACE: Come on, Rick.

PHIL: Okay, Ricky, blow it by him. Why are *you* in here?

GRACE: We're in a pennant race. This is an important game.

PHIL: The season opened a week ago.

GRACE: Christ almighty, hangs the curve—

PHIL: Goes...foul. I mean, it's April.

GRACE: You should see me in September. When people start to say, "What happened to this season?" I'll be thinking, "Remember that close one back in April?" It comes back to *me*.

PHIL: Ohhh. When you said this was an important game, you didn't mean compared to other games, you meant compared to everything else.

GRACE: I meant it was a game of *baseball*. They're probably about to leave, huh?

PHIL: After this inning we'll throw rice at Cindy.

GRACE: They're using rose petals.

PHIL: I bet if you ball those up real tight, you could throw them pretty hard.

GRACE: Now you're talking. Come on, Rick, ground ball to the left.

PHIL: Throw the double-play ball.

GRACE: Yes!

PHIL: Six! To four!

GRACE: Pivots! Throws!

PHIL: To three!

GRACE: Digs it out!

PHIL: Double play!

GRACE: God above, that's a beautiful thing.

(The lights crossfade as they cross toward the car.)

PHIL: You want to maybe—

GRACE: Yeah, we'd better.

PHIL: I'm Phil, in case you—

GRACE: Grace. Hi.

(The lights change to:)

Scene Two

(Car interior, daylight. Engine sounds and wind. PHIL is driving. GRACE is crouched, contorted, in the back seat, attempting to remove a very large dress without being seen by passing cars. This is difficult.)

PHIL: Huh.

GRACE: Did you say something?

PHIL: No.

GRACE: I'm gonna kill Julia.

PHIL: We'll get there.

GRACE: In a scarlet taffeta ballgown with great big sweat stains.

PHIL: So take it off, put it back on when we get there.

GRACE: What the hell do you think I'm doing back here, Greco-Roman wrestling? Have you ever tried getting out of three crinoline skirts in a compact car?

PHIL: No.

GRACE: You haven't lived.

PHIL: So I've been thinking about what you said.

GRACE: Which?

PHIL: When you look at someone you care about.

GRACE: What, like at weddings?

PHIL: Yeah. How come that's never happened to me before?

GRACE: Couldn't tell you.

PHIL: Huh. So I told you I ran into Cathy?

(All motion ceases in the back seat. GRACE pokes her head up.)

GRACE: No, you didn't.

PHIL: Didn't I? Sure, I did.

GRACE: Nooo, I would have remembered.

PHIL: Oh. Well, I did. She dropped off the last of my stuff.

GRACE: Nice of her.

PHIL: Yeah, I was surprised.

GRACE: Then what happened?

PHIL: Oh, you know. I've been trying to figure out why she and I didn't work out. I mean, I'm glad we didn't, obviously, 'cause....

GRACE: Because...?

PHIL: But I think I took it harder than I thought.

(GRACE cautiously goes back to changing.)

GRACE: You were together how long?

PHIL: Hang on...ten days.

GRACE: Ten—

PHIL: Wait, is that right?

GRACE: How did I get the idea that Cathy was a major relationship?

PHIL: She was.

GRACE: I've had colds that lasted longer.

PHIL: We lived together.

GRACE: How long, a week?

PHIL: About. Look, it's a long story.

GRACE: Can't be that long.

PHIL: I moved in on our anniversary, and then, I don't know, the romance went out of it.

GRACE: So. Cathy came over...

PHIL: Gave me back my stuff, we talked over old times—

GRACE: Old times?

PHIL: Are you okay?

GRACE: I have a pounding headache.

PHIL: Have you taken something for it?

GRACE: No.

PHIL: Well, could you?

GRACE: In a minute. Are you sorry you and Cathy broke up?

PHIL: No! But I think it was two things. One was the day I got home and she asked me to pick the mattress off the kitchen floor and move it back to the bedroom. I understood, her Mom was coming over, but...I didn't care who knew.

GRACE: Why'd you move the bed into the kitchen?

PHIL: So there'd be one less reason to ever get up. Eating, working, sports, all that, bathroom breaks, I thought it ought to feel like we were still in bed. After that it was never the same.

GRACE: How old are you again?

PHIL: Twenty-seven.

GRACE: Okay, yeah. So that was the first thing, what was the second thing?

PHIL: We were driving home from Bob and Cindy's wedding and Cathy asked me did I notice that she had caught the bouquet and where Did I disappear to for so long and why did I give a high-five to the woman who knocked Cindy's hat off with a wad of rose petals.

(GRACE *grins and disappears behind the seat.*)

PHIL: It turned out that she doesn't like baseball. *(He adjusts the rearview mirror downward.)*

GRACE: Hey. What are you doing?

PHIL: Looking at you.

GRACE: Eyes on the road, driver.

PHIL: You know? Maybe there was a third thing. I thought I was in love with her. But...when I looked at her...

GRACE: Which I gather was mostly from *very* close up—

PHIL: I just looked at her. I didn't picture her from any other times.

GRACE: Not a lot of other times to choose from.

PHIL: Huh. So you think I've never done that 'cause I haven't loved anyone *long* enough. *(He's looking at her.)* But that can't be why, because...

(GRACE *leaves the car and enters a different light. She has on a nice blouse and skirt and wears an I D tag with a store logo.)*

GRACE: Look out!

(A baseball comes flying through the fourth wall. GRACE ducks out of the way. The roar of the crowd, the crack of the bat. Bright lights, strongly frontal. She is in a skybox in the Hubert Humphrey Metrodome. PHIL scrambles after the ball and joins her.)

PHIL: Holy shit!

GRACE: How did he do that!

(PHIL retrieves the ball and holds it up.)

PHIL: Right here! Gladden! Right here!

GRACE: *(Adrenalined)* That was a foul tip! He didn't even get good wood on the ball and it flies all the way into a skybox! I've seen a million foul balls, but you're in this living room, it's like he hit it out of the T V.

PHIL: Having a good time so far?

GRACE: Beats the hell out of what I usually do after work. Does this always happen, you walk through the door and they hit a ball in your lap?

PHIL: Ah, you get used to it. I'm kidding, you think I rate this all the time? Marketing reserved it, cancelled at the last minute, Jack my boss had dibs, he's out of town, so I grabbed it. Do you want some food?

(GRACE unclips her I D tag and slips it in a pocket as she looks down at the crowd.)

GRACE: Not right now. *(She does a double-take.)* Hey, that—

PHIL: What?

GRACE: Nothing, no way, sorry.

PHIL: You okay?

GRACE: My brain must be fried. All the old people in baseball caps—sheesh, that weirds me out—I thought I saw my Mom.

PHIL: Does she go to a lot of games?

GRACE: She died years ago.

PHIL: Oh. Huh.

GRACE: What?

PHIL: No, just—"If you build it, she will—"

GRACE: Oh, shut up. So is it gonna be just us?

PHIL: I left a bunch of messages. Pretty short notice, though.

GRACE: Will—sorry, I don't remember her name—will she be here? Your date at the wedding.

PHIL: Cathy. No. We broke up, actually.

GRACE: Oh. I'm—The wedding was five days ago, when did this happen?

PHIL: Five days ago.

GRACE: Oh. Yikes.

(PHIL *holds up a Twins baseball cap.*)

PHIL: Hey. Do you think this'll fit a four-year-old girl? I haven't seen her in a while, but it seems really big.

GRACE: Should be okay. Who's it for?

PHIL: My niece. *(He pulls out other souvenirs.)* The pennants are for the nephews. Check out the Twins romper suit.

GRACE: How many nieces and nephews do you have?

(PHIL *reaches for his wallet and flips through pictures.*)

PHIL: These are my brother's kids—Joshua, he's five, he's in accelerated kindergarten, and Jason, he's three, he's supposed to look like me but I don't see it. Here's my sister's kids—Jody's the four-year-old, she just hit the horsey stage, and Jeremiah's about to be one.

(GRACE *isn't looking at the pictures, she's looking at* PHIL.)

GRACE: You like children.

PHIL: Well...sure, you know. *(He glances fondly at the pictures and puts the wallet away.)*

GRACE: Oh, come on.

PHIL: What?

GRACE: Cut it out, seriously.

PHIL: What?

GRACE: Nothing. Never mind.

(Pause)

PHIL: I can't believe nobody else has shown up.

GRACE: It does seem strange, yeah.

(Pause)

PHIL: Oh! Okay. Jeez, I'm an idiot! You think I set this up. I told you there'd be a crowd and so far it's only me. You're thinking what if it's a date and you didn't know! I feel like an idiot!

GRACE: You feel—I walk in the door and in two minutes' time you tell me you're unattached and you love kids. How am I supposed to feel? I mean, Jesus, I'm only thirty-four, I'm not standing outside the sperm bank with a little tin cup just yet.

(Pause)

PHIL: You're thirty-four?

GRACE: Say well-preserved or anything like it, you're a dead man.

PHIL: Did some guy do something to you that I should know about so I don't even start to do it?

GRACE: No one in particular. Do you think it would take the exceptional cruelty of one particular man to make me a little cautious?

(Uh-oh. GRACE and PHIL turn quickly back to the game.)

PHIL: Aaand Gladden gets the base on balls.

(Long awkward pause. Then GRACE *does a double-take.)*

GRACE: Lord! Do you ever have one of those days where everyone you see, you mistake them for somebody you know? There's no way my Dad's here.

PHIL: Is he dead, too?

GRACE: No, but he only went to games on all his visitation days with me.

PHIL: You luckout.

GRACE: I asked him once did he think there was any chance Harmon Killebrew was my real father.

PHIL: Ow. What did he do?

GRACE: He said he wouldn't be a bit surprised. God, was I a stinker.

PHIL: Hey. Help me out here. You would know this.

GRACE: What?

PHIL: Who is that?

GRACE: Chuck Knoblauch. Rookie, second base.

PHIL: I know. But what you were saying. Who *is* that?

GRACE: Who does he remind you—?

PHIL: Whose batting stance is that?

GRACE: You're right—

PHIL: Charlie Lau style—

GRACE: Yeah, the head, but look at the wrists.

PHIL: Vertical bat, head down, who is that?

GRACE: Why am I thinking Red Sox?

PHIL: Yes!

GRACE: Boggs? No.

PHIL: Greenwell.

GRACE: You think?

PHIL: No.

GRACE: Jody—?

PHIL: Jody Reed.

GRACE: It's Jody Reed.

PHIL: Plain as day.

GRACE: Huh. Everybody's here.

(PHIL *puts up his hand.* GRACE *slaps it in a high-five. Their hands stay attached. They're still looking at each other. The crowd roars.*)

PHIL: Watch it!

(PHIL *and* GRACE *duck out of the way as a baseball comes flying through the fourth wall.* PHIL *goes scrambling after it.*)

GRACE: Jesus!

PHIL: Yes! Amazing!

GRACE: Jesus Christ!

(PHIL *retrieves the ball and holds it up to wave to the crowd.*)

PHIL: Chuck! You god! I want your autograph!

(*The crowd roars.*)

GRACE: What are the odds that it—what are the—

PHIL: This is why you come to the park!

GRACE: Jesus H—

PHIL: The game is live!

GRACE: Right by our—

PHIL: We are live!

(*The lights fade fast.*)

Scene Three

(Car interior, daylight. Engine sounds and wind)

PHIL: Are you okay?

GRACE: Been better.

PHIL: I didn't know you got carsick.

GRACE: Me neither. There, Highway 210, that's our next turn, one mile. Great, only one and a half pages of Julia's goddamn directions to go.

PHIL: So I want to ask you about something.

GRACE: Okay.

PHIL: And I need you to try not to get angry.

GRACE: I'll try.

PHIL: Because it's kind of complicated.

GRACE: I'll try, all *right*? Highway 210, three quarters of a mile.

PHIL: Got it.

GRACE: So talk to me.

PHIL: Okay. I really like you.

GRACE: Well. I really like you, too.

PHIL: Okay. That's great. Okay.

GRACE: Is this about Cathy?

PHIL: Kind of.

GRACE: I knew it.

PHIL: And other people, too.

GRACE: Other women.

PHIL: Yeah. No, God, not "other women" like The Other Woman, just—women. From the past.

GRACE: Dolley Madison? Mamie Eisenhower?

PHIL: I'm trying to tell you something that's painful and revealing for me to say, and we thank you for your support!

GRACE: I'm sorry. Half a mile to Highway 210. You were saying.

PHIL: Maybe another time.

GRACE: Tell me now. Please.

PHIL: You've got to let me concentrate a little. Don't get angry right away?

GRACE: Go ahead.

PHIL: See, when it comes to women—

GRACE: Already I'm angry.

PHIL: I just started.

GRACE: Swell.

PHIL: I'm trying to be honest with you.

GRACE: Well, thank God for *that*, I mean thank God that the horrible statement I see on the horizon here isn't a *fabrication*.

PHIL: So when it comes to women, I—

GRACE: Phil? When speaking to a woman, try not to say, "When it comes to women." Quarter of a mile, coming right up.

PHIL: When it comes to...my relationships. I think I've gotten way too...goal-oriented. There's a checklist by now. First glance and look away. First talk. First laugh. First little flirtation. First phone call, first lunch, first heavy conversation. First date, first touch, first kiss, first dance, first awful true confession. First day together, sleep together, night together, morning together, meeting each others' friends together, first big fight. First screaming multiple orgasm—

GRACE: *Thank* you okay. Thank you for sharing. These women. Once you've done these things. What happens?

PHIL: That's the thing. After that I run out of ideas.

GRACE: You run out of ideas. That's the list.

PHIL: Pretty much.

GRACE: And after that, after *that* list—

PHIL: I'm sure I left out a few things.

GRACE: Hoo boy. And now?

PHIL: Now?

GRACE: Yeah.

PHIL: I guess I'm wondering what's the point.

GRACE: Shit. Did we exit?

PHIL: What?

GRACE: Did you take the exit?

PHIL: I think so.

GRACE: I don't think you did. You drove right by it.

PHIL: I was trying to put something important into words.

GRACE: Fine, that's great, now put the car into reverse.

PHIL: Did it make sense, what I was—

GRACE: It made perfect sense, now turn the car around!

PHIL: I'll turn around when I get another exit! I'll be taking Highway 210, right?

GRACE: 210 East.

PHIL: Great. West, though, right? 'Cause we're coming from the other way.

GRACE: We still have to go east.

PHIL: That's right. But it's a left now.

GRACE: Right.

PHIL: Okay. So. After Cathy and I broke up, I thought, great, fine, I'll just find somebody else.

GRACE: Can we stop for a moment to consider all the assumptions behind "I'll just find somebody else?"

PHIL: Sure. I go out, I drink, play games, watch sports, go to work, find somebody else. There are a lot of Cathies out there. Then what? It used to be an adventure to meet someone new. Lately it's a commute.

GRACE: And now...

PHIL: I really like you.

GRACE: Right, got that, good.

PHIL: And I don't know what to do.

GRACE: Do.

PHIL: Yeah.

GRACE: Oh God. Okay. Yeah. It's been great. We'll talk sometime.

PHIL: No, see—

GRACE: No, you're right, we won't talk sometime. We won't do a thing, this is it, you've run out of ideas. You were a person I wanted to be with and meanwhile I'm a bunch of things you wanted to do.

PHIL: I knew you'd get angry.

GRACE: Get out. Get out of here.

PHIL: We're going seventy miles an hour.

GRACE: Better yet.

PHIL: What did I do?

GRACE: One: You're getting us lost. Two: You're trying to break something to me, and I wish you'd get it over with.

PHIL: One: I am turning around. Two: I'm not trying to break anything to you, I'm saying I don't know what to do about how I feel.

GRACE: Fine, I heard that.

PHIL: So I'm asking for suggestions.

GRACE: You call that a list? Me and some guys have gotten through that list in a weekend.

PHIL: Huh.

GRACE: You want some real goals, Phil? When does he start talking to me every day? When does he stop wanting to see anybody else? When does he meet my godawful family? When does he start making some plans? When does he want to change his life? What if something happens?

(Pause)

PHIL: So you think I have the wrong list.

GRACE: It's a wee bit limited.

PHIL: Huh. I was thinking what's wrong was having a list.

(GRACE turns to look at him. She smiles. The lights start to change. Music comes in, low: a small band playing a big band dance tune.)

PHIL: 'Cause I think what I'm trying to say is—

GRACE: Uh-oh.

(GRACE snaps her head to the front. The lights and sound snap back to normal.)

PHIL: You okay?

GRACE: Yeah. My eyes were just...weird. *(She's trying to not look quite at him.)* Look, before I hear any more I'm gonna need to find a drugstore. Okay?

PHIL: Sure. 'Cause I think we missed the exit again.

GRACE: Oh, for God's sake.

PHIL: I'm sorry.

GRACE: No, I'm sorry. I should have planned better, I shouldn't have picked today to feel so cruddy, you're being—very nice.

PHIL: I'm having a good time.

GRACE: I'm not always like this, you know? We've had fun sometimes.

PHIL: We have.

GRACE: I'll be more fun again soon.

PHIL: Relax. You're giving me a chance to feel relatively mature.

GRACE: *(Giving him a look)* You? You wish.

(The lights and music come up again. PHIL crosses downstage onto a dance floor, doing a formless sort of freestyle boogaloo.)

PHIL: I love dancing! You'd never know it to look at me.

(GRACE crosses to him. She is wearing another godawful bridesmaid's gown.)

PHIL: I still think that's a nice dress.

GRACE: I'm gonna kill Shelley.

PHIL: Hey, it's 'way better than the thing Cindy made you wear.

GRACE: You told me you liked that.

PHIL: Well, I like this better. It looks nice on you.

GRACE: Friendship is based on trust.

PHIL: I meant that I like your shoulders.

GRACE: Oh. By the way, this is a tango. What are you doing?

PHIL: That's amazing. You know an actual dance?

GRACE: It's just a tango. Like this. *(She dances for a couple of bars, well.)* Nobody ever sent you to dance class?

PHIL: I don't know anyone who can do a dance with a name.

GRACE: Oh, come on.

PHIL: Look around the room. Huh? Disaster area.

GRACE: I got sent to these classes where we learned steps to music that no one with a brain would play anymore. Jesus, I feel like the chaperone.

PHIL: Teach it to me.

GRACE: This is embarrassing.

PHIL: You could try. Come on.

GRACE: Okay, come here. And...

(They try, and fail.)

PHIL: Tell you what. You do the tango and I'll do what I do.

(GRACE and PHIL do: she tangos across the floor as he dances freestyle around her, shaping the space around her and making "tah-dah" gestures behind her moves. She has trouble keeping a straight face.)

GRACE: You're not supposed to smile when you do the tango.

(PHIL's dance assumes a few tangolike poses. GRACE makes a few "tah-dah" moves.)

PHIL: Yes! The Kid is dancing!

(The music ends. Clapping)

GRACE: The Kid?

PHIL: Me, sort of. Thing I do. It's kind of dumb.

GRACE: Tell me.

PHIL: Like, if I've got dishes to do, I'll say, "The Kid is stepping up to the sink, Red! He's using Lemon Joy and a wood-handled brush in there, Vin. Would you look at the scrubbing technique on the Kid!"

GRACE: Why "the Kid?"

PHIL: It's what my Dad used to call me. I turned it into something fun.

GRACE: I've heard of making up imaginary playmates. You made Up E S P N.

PHIL: My brother and sister are way older than me. I think I was an accident. Something my Dad said.... I asked my Mom, and she said, "Maybe an accident, but certainly not a mistake."

GRACE: Yay, Mom.

PHIL: Yeah, good save. Anyway, I played alone a lot.

(A mirror ball descends and is hit by colored lights. The band starts a slow one.)

GRACE: Oh, my God...

PHIL: Awright! Slow dance!

GRACE: I'm with a sixteen-year-old.

(GRACE and PHIL start doing a waltz-type thing, which gradually decays into the swaying vertical hug of high-school dances. He grins at her. She looks at him.)

GRACE: What?

PHIL: What?

GRACE: What am I doing funny?

PHIL: Nothing. What am I doing?

GRACE: You're grinning again.

PHIL: *(Trying to straighten his face)* Still?

GRACE: Not so much.

PHIL: Now? Better?

(GRACE *and* PHIL *are looking at each other with very serious expressions. She begins to crack first, which starts him, and she makes a little sputtery sound, and it's all over, they're grinning and laughing. Then they just look at each other.)*

PHIL: Wow.

GRACE: Hm. You know, we could—

PHIL: I bet we could.

GRACE: Yeah?

PHIL: Oh, yeah.

(GRACE *and* PHIL *look around and stealthily sidle away, back toward the car. As they go, the lights crossfade to:)*

Scene Four

(Daylight. GRACE *and* PHIL *in the car.)*

GRACE: No!

PHIL: What!

GRACE: Look at the road signs.

PHIL: What?

GRACE: Half the words are French.

PHIL: Huh.

GRACE: Tell me we're not in Canada, Phil.

PHIL: No way.

GRACE: Canada or New Orleans, take your pick. Phil, we are seriously lost. We're not gonna make it. God, what is Julia gonna think?

PHIL: Do you have a number where the wedding's going to be?

GRACE: I called from the drugstore, I got a machine.

PHIL: This is ridiculous. They expect you to find this place in the middle of the wilderness, you're sick as a dog, it's probably over already.

GRACE: Plus we've been driving in every direction but the right one for hours.

PHIL: What do you want to do? You want me to drive you home?

GRACE: I hate to break it to you, Phil, but what I want is for you to ask someone for directions.

PHIL: Aw, hell.

GRACE: *(Moaning)* Oh. Oh God.

PHIL: Still feeling bad?

GRACE: Uh-huh.

PHIL: What did you get at the drugstore, didn't it help?

GRACE: Uh-uh.

PHIL: *(Pointing)* Here! What you need is some solid food. Soft drink, fix you right up. Huh? We'll go to the drive-thru window. Do you know what you want?

GRACE: I want to die.

PHIL: I'll order first.

(A preposterous plastic cartoon thing with a speaker inside appears next to the car. PHIL leans out the window.)

PHIL: Hi!

(Unintelligible static)

PHIL: Uh, howdy. Could I get a western bacon double cheeseburger, and, let's see, the ranch-style fries—

(GRACE is quietly overcome by a feral alertness, going very still except for her eyes.)

PHIL: —that's a large, and some extra barbeque sauce with that would be great. Grace? You know what you want? Mushroom burger?

GRACE: Start without me. (*She grabs her purse and exits fast.*)

PHIL: Grace? I think my friend is heading inside, I'll come in for it, all right? Listen, is there anything on the menu you'd recommend for somebody with an upset stomach? McSoda Crackers or something?

(*A toilet flushes. The lights crossfade to:*)

(GRACE *is standing in the restroom. Hard, fluorescent lights, sound of running water and through the wall the clash of kitchen trays. In one hand she is holding, gingerly, the small plastic cup and testing stick from a pregnancy test kit. The cup is full. In the other hand she holds the instructions, which she is reading with fierce concentration.*)

GRACE: Please. Please. Shit, Grace, who are you talking to? (*She looks around and shrinks a little. She takes a deep breath, pulls the testing stick from the cup, and watches it.*) Just—please. Be pink. Okay? Please. Not pregnant. Hey, little guy. Don't be blue? Huh? Be pink. And then later, you know? Later you can be anything you want. Just be pink for me now. Huh? Huh? Come on, you can tell I'm not ready for this, I'm talking to plastic. Which is Dodger blue. God damn it! I don't even know what country I'm in. How did this happen?

(*Seductive music.* GRACE *watches as* PHIL *enters, dragging a mattress with a bottomsheet, a couple of pillows, and a comforter.*)

GRACE: Okay, right. It comes back to me.

(*Lights down on* GRACE *as* PHIL *pulls off his shirt and necktie. He hops on one foot, as he kicks his shoes off. The bridesmaid's dress comes flying in. He undoes his pants.*)

(GRACE *strolls on, wrapped in a sheet, and meets* PHIL *at the foot of the mattress. He takes one corner of the sheet, and she does a pirouette, unwinding it. They are both upstage of the sheet.*)

GRACE: *(To the music)* Two, three—

(GRACE *and* PHIL *fall onto the mattress together, landing in positions of postcoital languor. After a moment, he leans up wearily on an elbow and gropes for a roll of toilet paper. He tears some off, reaches under the covers, makes a face, gives a pull and a couple of swabs. The hand reemerges with the paper in a crumpled ball.*)

PHIL: The Kid steps to the free throw line, he sets his stance... *(He tosses the ball of tissue offstage.)* Swish! The Kid completes the three-point play and we're going to overtime!

(GRACE *rolls toward* PHIL *and makes a face.*)

GRACE: Man, that stuff gets cold in a hurry.

PHIL: Don't look at me, mine are in the trash trying to impregnate a condom—

(GRACE *peeks under the top sheet.*)

GRACE: No way this is all me.

PHIL: —I picture them beating their tiny heads against the walls, going, *(He pulls the top sheet tightly over his head.)* "Grace! Grace! Grace!"

GRACE: I was really having a time.

PHIL: Hi.

GRACE: Mmmm.

PHIL: How are you?

GRACE: Hee hee hee.

PHIL: Really?

GRACE: Hee hee hee hee hee.

PHIL: That's, uh...

GRACE: Yeah?

PHIL: This has been a very pleasant evening and I'm not just saying that.

(GRACE *and* PHIL *chortle.*)

PHIL: Did you doze off?

GRACE: God, I must have.

PHIL: Can I imagine that you passed out cold?

GRACE: Whatever.

(PHIL *holds up a hand.*)

PHIL: Big high-five for the Kid?

GRACE: There are times I envy you so much it could kill me.

PHIL: I've done something wrong here. I can tell.

GRACE: You're not wrong, but.... Yes you are. You're wrong. I come more than once, it's a tribute to *you.* Mister Prowess *made* me come. *You* come more than once, it's also a tribute to you.

PHIL: I have this concern about...I just want you to be pleased.

GRACE: I was pleased. Really pleased.

(*Pause*)

PHIL: I've been thinking. How would you feel about moving in together?

GRACE: Phil. That is an incredibly sweet suggestion.

PHIL: That isn't a "yes," I guess, huh?

GRACE: You want to get through a woman as quick as you can, don'tcha?

PHIL: What do you mean?

GRACE: Sweetie, you've been *thinking* about this? Since when? Five seconds ago? Ten? It's just... Most people, they talk about moving in together, it's a commitment. With you, it's a second date. What's the rush?

PHIL: I guess.

GRACE: Have I hurt your feelings?

PHIL: No. I'm okay.

GRACE: Listen, I'd better get going. If I stay here longer, Mister Prowess will render me useless for the workday.

PHIL: Yeah?

GRACE: Get some sleep. And thank you for a lovely time. You pile-driving marathon sex god.

PHIL: Look at the sexual technique on the Kid!

(GRACE *laughs, and starts gathering up her clothes.*)

PHIL: What's he using in there, Red? Well, those are male genitalia, Vin. The Kid is earning some big bucks from product endorsements for those genitals, isn't he, Red? Yes, Vin, and it's a disturbing trend, teenagers are shooting each other over those penises.... You don't have to go.

GRACE: I have to get to work in a few hours.

PHIL: So do I, so? Blow it off.

GRACE: Come on.

PHIL: I mean it.

GRACE: Walk me to my car?

(GRACE *starts to get dressed.* PHIL's *staring into space. She stops, and looks at him.*)

GRACE: Phil? How are things at work?

PHIL: Oh, Lordy.

GRACE: Phil? How's work, Phil?

PHIL: Work. Work has been kind of...not. *(He starts getting dressed.)*

GRACE: Phil. You didn't.

PHIL: You know what they wanted me to do? Last week I met with the people on one of our assembly floors to tell them about their wonderful new flexible benefit plan. This week my boss wanted me to go back and tell them about their severance pay. Every one of those guys would have thought I knew all along they were screwed.

GRACE: Did you know?

PHIL: No! My boss has stopped telling me stuff in advance. He knows I'm a bad liar, so he doesn't trust me anymore.

GRACE: So you quit.

PHIL: No—

GRACE: You made a big fiery speech to your boss and you quit.

PHIL: I made a big fiery speech to the mirror and called in sick.

GRACE: What are you going to do?

PHIL: I'll get another job.

GRACE: You'll just get another—nobody's getting other jobs!

PHIL: I always have.

GRACE: Always? Have you done this kind of thing a lot?

PHIL: My jobs always go bad. It's awful.

GRACE: What?

PHIL: It's just.... They keep promoting me.

GRACE: Promoting you.

PHIL: Yeah. Raises, bigger office, perks.

GRACE: The bastards.

PHIL: The more they promote me, the tougher they need me to be. At first it's following rotten orders, then it's thinking up rotten ideas of your own. I've tried, I really have, but...I feel like I'm letting them down. Finally I go somewhere else.

GRACE: You're in personnel, and you think you can just go somewhere else? I'm in retail, I see what's going on. I used to spend my day saying, "Will there be anything else? Do you need some stockings to go with that?" Now I tell people, "I'm sorry, but the credit card company informs me that I must confiscate and destroy your card."

PHIL: Wow. What do they do?

GRACE: A lot of them try to grab it back.

PHIL: They come after you?

GRACE: It helps if you pick up the scissors before you tell them. Once you cut their name in two they kind of...deflate.

PHIL: I bet you could get another job.

GRACE: Jesus, Phil! This is what I'm trying to get through your skull! When a job like mine comes open, the line goes around the block! Don't you interview job applicants? Can't you see how desperate they are?

PHIL: They are at first, but I tell them their résumé looks good—and it does, their résumés all look amazingly good—I say we'll keep them in mind, and they cheer up.

GRACE: Oh. Don't ever do that. Phil, you shouldn't ever do that.

PHIL: Why not?

GRACE: You're getting their hopes up. You're not going to hire those people.

PHIL: We might.

GRACE: But you won't.

PHIL: We should.

GRACE: But you won't. Don't tell people something just to get their hopes up. It's a rotten thing to do. *(Pause)* The bathroom is this way?

PHIL: Yeah.

(As GRACE goes, PHIL wistfully picks up the mattress and drags it off. She turns and watches him as the lights crossfade to:)

Scene Five

(Daylight. GRACE and PHIL sit on the hood of the car. She looks miserable. He is eating a burger and watching her.)

PHIL: I wish you'd tell me why you're upset.

GRACE: What makes you think I'm upset? I've dropped the ball on a major commitment to Julia, I'm out a lot of money for a dress I never even wore, I'm lost, I'm standing in a parking lot in an overcoat and my underwear, I'm—sick.... You got some tissues?

PHIL: Somewhere in there.

(GRACE leans into the car and feels between the seat cushions. Her face crumples a bit and she sniffs loudly.)

PHIL: Are you crying?

GRACE: No.

PHIL: Are you sure?

GRACE: I have an allergy.

PHIL: To what?

GRACE: To people asking me a lot of questions when I'm crying. *(She grabs a hunk of red taffeta dress and blows her nose on that.)*

PHIL: Is this 'cause we missed the wedding?

GRACE: I hate weddings. A wedding is designed to make the bride feel good about getting married by humiliating all the single women there. By the time she throws the bouquet, I don't want to catch the thing, I want to shoot it out of the sky. I'm sorry. I'll have a good cry and I'll be better in a minute or two.

PHIL: A good *cry*? A *good* cry? This is scaring the bejesus out of me. Can I do anything to help?

GRACE: *(Smiling a little)* You want to help me cry?

PHIL: I want to help you stop.

(GRACE looks at PHIL. She touches his face.)

GRACE: You're a nice boy, Phil. You're a lot of fun.

(Pause)

PHIL: What do you want to do?

GRACE: Nothing.

PHIL: Where do you want to go?

GRACE: I don't care.

PHIL: Hey. Now you're talking. Hitting the road!

(PHIL jumps in the car and guns the motor as GRACE climbs in.)

PHIL: This is great, in a way.

GRACE: In what possible way is this great?

PHIL: It's almost as good as a road trip.

GRACE: What's a road trip?

PHIL: What. Is a *road trip*?

GRACE: Some kind of vacation?

PHIL: Vacation? No *way*. A vacation is valet parking and how much do we tip the maid.

GRACE: Those are bad things?

PHIL: A road trip is when you get in a car and see where you wind up. The great thing is not to know where you're going till you're just about there.

GRACE: How do you decide?

PHIL: You get an omen.

GRACE: An omen.

PHIL: Okay, we're driving along, taking likely looking roads—

GRACE: Likely looking?

PHIL: Say you're telling personal history stories, and up ahead you can turn onto, One: a freeway; or Two: a slow back road where you can see the moon. What's your choice?

GRACE: Back road?

PHIL: Exactly. But if you've got a Chuck Berry song on the radio?

GRACE: Freeway?

PHIL: That's it.

GRACE: You're going along, you're talking—

PHIL: Maybe you've got a game on the radio, junk food around your feet—junk food is very important—

GRACE: For energy?

PHIL: Atmosphere. I don't know—it only works if it's coming out of really garbagey circumstances.

GRACE: Game on the radio...

PHIL: Rock and roll, something. Okay, for instance: it's evening, you're driving through the outskirts of Indianapolis—this really happened—the sky's gone weird and it's affecting the radio reception, it's pulled in some sports roundup talk show, and they mention the Yankees are opening a home stand against the Red Sox the next day. And right that second, a line of businessmen gets off the bus ahead of you, all wearing pinstripe suits. What do you do?

GRACE: Pinstripes. The Yankees wear pinstripes.

PHIL: At home.

GRACE: You drive to New York.

PHIL: Yes! Yes! That is what you do! You drive all night, you take turns at the wheel, and sleep in the back seat. You get to the Bronx, you see the game, you drive back.

GRACE: You burn a lot of fossil fuel.

PHIL: You pull back into your street after a drive like that, you've done something.

GRACE: Something kind of goofy.

PHIL: Sure it's goofy, but what you've done is you know someone. You spend a few days with somebody in a space no bigger than this, you know who they are. You get a lot of thinking done.

(Pause)

GRACE: One: I have to buy some human clothing. Two: I need to be back for work tomorrow morning.

PHIL: Yes! Yes! You're gonna love this!

(PHIL races the engine. GRACE turns on the radio and searches the dial. He watches her.)

PHIL: Wow...

GRACE: What?

PHIL: You know what's great? Your back, between your shoulders. There's a curve.

GRACE: Watch the road.

PHIL: No, though, it's—your neck curves in, then out for your shoulders and then in again.

GRACE: I'm hunchbacked, you're saying.

PHIL: Bannh. Wrong. But *here's* what it is: that curve is because you have another set of curves that start at one shoulder and go across your shoulderblade and dip into your spine and out and up the shoulderblade on the other side and across that shoulder. So you've got these curves this way meeting across these curves running this other way. It's...harmonious.

GRACE: I feel like this *thing* now.

PHIL: You know, I could look at this back for a long time. *(A deep breath)* 'Cause I think what I'm trying to say is—

GRACE: Whoa. Slow down a sec.

PHIL: What?

GRACE: This...really isn't fair. Okay? You waltz around praising my body and wiping my nose and it isn't fair, so stop, okay? Please. Just stop.

PHIL: Stop what?

GRACE: You can't possibly keep this up. And right about the time I start getting used to all this...right when I start needing this...this...

PHIL: Well. Love, actually. And he says it! *(He honks the horn a few times.)*

GRACE: Oh, this is bad.

PHIL: It's taken me the whole damn day!

GRACE: This is gonna be so bad.

PHIL: How are you feeling? You feeling any better?

GRACE: Wait a minute—are you saying you love me as a way of cheering me *up*?

PHIL: Doesn't it?

GRACE: You want to cheer someone up, you say, "There, there," you say, "Poor sweet baby." You don't make a life-changing announcement.

PHIL: Why not?

GRACE: Because "There, there" and "Poor sweet baby" don't *mean* anything. They're just noises people make. I worry that "I love you" is just this *noise* you're making.

PHIL: It's not.

GRACE: How do I know that?

PHIL: I'm telling you.

GRACE: Okay. I have to tell you something.

PHIL: Is this to do with why what I said didn't make you happy?

GRACE: *(Very unhappily)* I'm happy, Phil. It's scary, that's all. Anyway, yeah. It's some not necessarily really good news.

PHIL: I thought there was something on your mind. Anyway, I know all about it.

GRACE: What do you know?

PHIL: I got a call from Kyle. He told me he and Suzannah split up.

GRACE: My God.

PHIL: They haven't even gotten the credit card bills from the honeymoon.

GRACE: It's awful.

PHIL: Yeah, it is. But you're not Suzannah. Okay? I'm not Kyle. We're gonna be all right.

GRACE: Well, good. Good, I mean, I'm glad I didn't have to break it to you, that...really bad news, about... them. *(Pause)* I wonder.... Suzannah wanted to start a family right away. Boy, I wonder if she's pregnant.

PHIL: That would be pretty awful.

GRACE: You think so.

PHIL: Sure. What would she do?

(Pause)

GRACE: Basically she would have five options.

PHIL: Five—

GRACE: I'm just talking off the top of my head, here, but.... One: They split up for good and she has it and raises it alone—

PHIL: Can you picture that? "Son, this is your father. He and I were married for a couple of weeks a few years back." Unless she has a ton of money—

GRACE: *(To herself)* Strike one.

PHIL: Or an understanding family—

GRACE: *(To herself)* Swinging strike two.

PHIL: I wouldn't wish it on anyone.

GRACE: Two: She decides to have it and they stay together—

PHIL: Trapped and resentful.

GRACE: Rrright. Three: She decides not to have it—

PHIL: Which is of course her choice—

GRACE: For the moment, yes.

PHIL: But it's a sad thing to have to do, especially if she thinks she's running out of chances, I mean Suzannah must be, what—

GRACE: Thirty-four.

PHIL: Right.

GRACE: Four: They stay together, she has the abortion, and doesn't tell Kyle.

PHIL: That's her business. But what kind of marriage is that gonna be?

GRACE: Five: She doesn't have the baby and she doesn't have Kyle. Which leaves Suzannah with no good options.

PHIL: Poor Suzannah.

GRACE: Poor old Suzannah.

PHIL: You've given this a lot of thought, huh.

GRACE: Yeah.

PHIL: How come?

(Pause)

GRACE: Well. Even when you use protection, there's a danger. *(Pause)* And I was late this month. *(Pause)* So I thought I'd better see if I was pregnant. *(Pause)* But I'm not.

PHIL: Hunh.

(Blackout)

END OF ACT ONE

ACT TWO

Scene One

(PHIL *is driving. He's wearing cheap jeans, t-shirt, and sneakers, and a Minnesota Twins cap.* GRACE *is asleep in the back, out of sight.*)

PHIL: Grace? You awake? Hey, Grace?

(PHIL *turns on the radio. He flips through the static along the dial until he finds the song from the top of the show. The rhythm is a deep pounding and a higher, faster sound. He listens and taps the steering wheel. Then the vocal to the song comes in. The words are spoken. The voices are* GRACE's *and his.*)

GRACE: *(On the radio)* So I thought I'd better see if I was pregnant.

(PHIL *stares at the radio.*)

GRACE: I'd bet I'd bet I'd better see if I was pregnant.

(PHIL *glances into the back seat and then back at the radio.*)

GRACE: I thought I'd better see if I was pregnant. But I'm not.

PHIL: *(On the radio)* Hunh!

GRACE: Even when you use protection, there's a danger. There's a a a a danger. I thought I'd better see if I was pregnant.

PHIL: *(On the radio)* Grace! We're running late!

GRACE: I was late this month.

(PHIL *mouths the words with the radio, increasingly stunned.*)

GRACE: I was laaaaate this, late this month. I thought I'd better see if I was pregnant. But I'm not.

(PHIL *turns off the radio.*)

PHIL: Grace?

(GRACE, *very pregnant, lies on a towel in the sun, wearing nothing but a baseball jersey, shades, and nasty high heels. She's smoking a cigarette elaborately. Bad girl stuff.*)

GRACE: What is it, Phil?

PHIL: Who is he?

GRACE: Who's who?

PHIL: Whose baby is it? Is it mine?

GRACE: If you think it's yours, it's yours.

PHIL: Whose is it really?

GRACE: I told you. Come on, there's a chance it's yours.

PHIL: Grace, please.

GRACE: Don't get mad?

PHIL: I never get mad.

GRACE: Okay, it was Harmon Killebrew.

PHIL: No. When? Where?

GRACE: Fantasy Camp. Phil, it had nothing to do with you. It's just—Harmon is bigger than you, and stronger than you, and richer than you, and older than you.

PHIL: Way older than me.

GRACE: Still swings from the hips, though. Phil, he's a Hall of Famer.

PHIL: Why did it have to be Killebrew? He was my idol.

GRACE: I don't know, it was dark. It might have been
Rod Carew.

(Blackout)

Scene Two

*(Engines roar. The wind blows. Traffic whizzes by. On the
passenger side,* GRACE *opens her eyes and stretches. She is
dressed the same as* PHIL.*)*

GRACE: Where are we?

PHIL: I'm not looking at the map, I'm squinching up
my eyes so I can't see the signs, and I won't ask for
directions.

GRACE: Those are the rules?

PHIL: They're not rules, they're just part of the idea. A
big point of a road trip is flexibility, Grace. *(Pause)* Hey,
I told you I heard from my nieces and nephews?

GRACE: No, you didn't.

PHIL: Didn't I? Well, I did. My brother and sister
both called and put the kids on to thank me for the
Twins stuff I sent. Joshua thinks that because I live in
Minneapolis, Kirby Puckett must be a friend of mine.
What's great about being an uncle is I can say, "That's
right, Josh, he is. Who do you think taught him to hit?"
I mean, if I were his dad, I wouldn't say that kind of
thing. Wouldn't be responsible. If I were his dad, I'd
tell him the truth.

(Pause)

GRACE: Do you know where we're going yet? Seen
anything omenish?

PHIL: Not yet.

GRACE: What time is it?

PHIL: I'm trying not to look at my watch.

GRACE: Why not?

PHIL: It's a road trip. There's no itinerary.

GRACE: Now entering—

PHIL: Don't tell me!

GRACE: Phil, why don't I drive, and then you can put a blindfold on. 'Cause I get the feeling I'm watching you kidnap yourself.

PHIL: I can look at the signs or I can look at the scenery. Tell you what. You search for omens. I don't care where we wind up.

GRACE: There's a tree! Tree, tree, orchard, forest, Forest Hills! We should go to Forest Hills! Or Ann Arbor...

PHIL: Try not to press it.

GRACE: Grain silos...long row of mailboxes...herbicide billboard...

PHIL: Relax.

GRACE: Are there times you never find it?

PHIL: I guess so. Sure.

GRACE: How long does it usually take?

PHIL: We may be passing omens galore and you're not in the frame of mind to see them.

GRACE: Now wait, you didn't tell me about a frame of mind.

PHIL: It won't work if there's too much in your head.

GRACE: I'm supposed to have nothing on my mind.

PHIL: *(Pointedly)* Yeah. Like if something's weighing on your mind? We might never get anywhere.

(Pause)

GRACE: Phil. What you said this morning.

PHIL: That I love you.

GRACE: *Oh*, man.

PHIL: It's still true.

GRACE: Really. Several hours later.

PHIL: I would love you no matter what.

GRACE: You shouldn't say that.

PHIL: Why not?

GRACE: I think you don't know what it means. When you say that to somebody—it's not a weather report, okay? It's supposed to be a promise. Would you promise me something, Phil? One favor.

PHIL: Anything. Anything. I promise.

GRACE: Ah, Phil. That's the thing. How am I supposed to trust you, when you think you can promise me anything?

(Pause. PHIL turns on the radio and begins scanning through the staticky dial. GRACE is watching him. The lights change, and the sound changes to flipping television channels.)

(PHIL leaves the car and waddles down to slump on a sofa bathed in blue television light. Between the light and his couch-potato posture, he looks awful. He's pointing a remote control.)

PHIL: It said 3:05. Four, no, five, no—Grace! Where's the *T V Guide*?

GRACE: In your lap.

PHIL: Aw, jeez. Get it for me, willya? Eleven, no, E S P N, no—*T V Guide* said Twins game 3:05.

GRACE: That's last week's, Phil.

PHIL: Shit. Maybe somebody else is playing. *(He holds down the "channel up" button on the remote control and we*

get little snatches of programs going by.) Soap, soap, baby
animals, soap, news, Oprah—

GRACE: Men who can't read a T V schedule, next on
Oprah.

PHIL: Shut up! Huckleberry Hound, news, seventies
made-for-T V movie, okay! Tire commercial! Gotta be a
game.

GRACE: Phil? Where were you last night?

PHIL: Here we go. Jesus, wrestling! *(He holds down
the remote button again.)* Courtroom drama, standup
comedy, news, old movie, prevue guide, shopping
network, stock market, infomercial, what is this—
Geraldo, God on a stick, ancient sitcom, more God,
don't know don't care, scramble channel, scramble
channel, music video, scramble channel, music video,
all right! Aerobics on the beach!

GRACE: Change it.

PHIL: I'm exercising here!

GRACE: Change it.

PHIL: Scramble, scramble, weather, Congress, Spanish
soap, weather—God in heaven, two weather channels
and no baseball—*Sesame Street.* We're back to the top,
that's it. *(He turns off the set and stares out dumbly.)*

GRACE: Phil? Where were you?

PHIL: Hey! I don't ask where you go.

GRACE: I go to work.

PHIL: You wanted a kid. I said I'd always be there for
you, and here I am, yes? Our deal was you work, I stay
home with the baby. Yes?

GRACE: But, Phil—

PHIL: What?

GRACE: Phil? Where's the baby?

(Pause. PHIL *thinks hard.)*

GRACE: Phil?

PHIL: Hang on...

(Blackout)

Scene Three

(Engines, sunlight, wind. GRACE *and* PHIL *in the car.)*

GRACE: I want to thank you.

PHIL: For what?

GRACE: For this. The road trip. It's a good idea. You get a lot of thinking done.

PHIL: Hey.

GRACE: What?

PHIL: *(Pointing out the window) Look* at that. Oh, that is great.

GRACE: What?

PHIL: That. I love that.

GRACE: I don't even see what you're pointing at.

PHIL: The hillside above that farm. Those big red rocks—

GRACE: What about them?

PHIL: And the tips of whatever they've planted there—

GRACE: Wheat?

PHIL: Don't know, but—same red. See?

GRACE: Okay.

PHIL: Now look at the barn.

GRACE: Same red.

PHIL: I would do that. I would paint my barn in honor of those rocks and those plants. Look what they're doing!

GRACE: Maybe it didn't happen on purpose.

PHIL: Then there's a God.

GRACE: There's you, noticing.

PHIL: There he *is*! He's walking out of his house! Quick!

GRACE: What?

(PHIL honks the horn.)

PHIL: In a red! Flannel! Shirt! Hold the wheel.

GRACE: What?

(PHIL lets go of the wheel and leans way out the window. GRACE yelps and grabs the steering wheel.)

GRACE: Phil! Jesus Christ!

PHIL: You! Farm guy! You are a great man! I want your autograph!

(PHIL sits back down and puts his hands on the wheel again. GRACE's fingers are frozen on the wheel. He carefully pries them off. Her hands reflexively grab for the dashboard.)

GRACE: Never ever ever ever—

PHIL: What's wrong?

GRACE: Scenery. I nearly died for scenery.

PHIL: *Great* scenery.

GRACE: Come on. In the winter, you think he paints the barn white? Does the chores in a dress shirt? Where have you *been*, Phil?

PHIL: *(Grinning)* All your life?

GRACE: All yours. *(Pause).* So that was our omen?

PHIL: That? No.

GRACE: Wasn't it?

PHIL: No. I just liked it.

GRACE: When you do find an omen, can I get a sense of what your reaction is going to be?

PHIL: It varies.

GRACE: I've hurt your feelings.

PHIL: It's okay.

GRACE: No, it's not okay. Because when I do it you tend to sulk.

PHIL: Sulk?

GRACE: You practically hold your breath till your face turns blue.

PHIL: I call that being tough. Living with my secret pain.

GRACE: When John Wayne does it, we call it being tough. John Wayne does not practically stick out his lower lip as if to say, "Look at me living with my secret pain." That we call sulking.

PHIL: I wish someone had told me that before. I get the feeling there's a lot of things people don't tell me. *(He looks at her.)*

GRACE: Watch the road. *(Pause)* Phil, it's hard to tell you the truth, sometimes. The truth about things is so vastly inferior to what you seem to think is going on. It's hard to spoil your fun.

PHIL: You make me sound like I'm some kind of kid.

(GRACE just looks at PHIL.)

PHIL: Ow.

GRACE: Phil, in this world there are lovable people and there are unlovable people. You, Phil, are frighteningly lovable. You love the world and it loves you right back. You go through your day like a goddamn receiving line. "Hiya, Phil," say the plants. "Look over *here*,

Phil!" say the rocks. "Hey, Phil," says the barn, "How's our boy?"

PHIL: But—that's how people talk to a baby.

GRACE: Well. Everybody loves a baby.

PHIL: But they don't take him seriously. Do they.

(Pause)

GRACE: So what do you want to do—

PHIL: When I grow up? Hang out with you.

GRACE: How long?

PHIL: Indefinitely.

GRACE: Yeah. That's the thing.

PHIL: What do you want? For yourself?

GRACE: To watch the Twins win the pennant.

PHIL: Seriously. I mean, I know you're serious. But besides that. What do you picture?

GRACE: I'm thirty-four years old. I don't picture myself anymore. I see other people and wish that I could have been them.

PHIL: Why? I don't—this is what I cannot *get* about you. You say things that are so *sad*, about yourself, and—listen. You know what I love to do?

GRACE: Everything. Everything you do, you love to do.

PHIL: You've never seen me at work. I know you're supposed to have ambitions, but I just don't do anything in a champion caliber way. But what I love to do is to see great things. I don't need to do anything. I just love to know. I think the only thing I do really well is cheer. When you know something is really great, you can look at the people you're with and say, "You know what's great? That right there." When I'm alone with you, I always want to point and say, "You know what's great? That woman there." But the only other person in the room is booing all the time. Which can be hard. *(Pause)* This whole drive I've been looking at you and...doing that thing you said.

GRACE: What thing?

PHIL: I've been seeing all the times we've been together. I've never done this before in my life. I know I haven't loved you very long. But I think I love you in a lot of detail.

GRACE: Phil. The way you've been—seeing me today. There's a down side. When you—if you fall out of love, if it's bad, you—when you look at *yourself*—you see that awful time. And you have to be able to look at yourself again.... So you lose that part of your life.

PHIL: This happened to you.

GRACE: Ages twenty-three through twenty-seven inclusive. Pretty much gone. Meeting, courtship, marriage, divorce. Dim shapes, that's it.

PHIL: You've been married. You never told me.

GRACE: Not much left to tell.

PHIL: What was his name?

GRACE: Roy. His name was Roy. Is Roy, I guess, somewhere. Roy. I haven't said his name in years. Roy. What a dumb name.

PHIL: You really don't remember anything?

GRACE: I remember the facts, but...I can't feel it. I remember his nose. And...a fight we had in a café, he grabbed my arm. And standing on the platform in the cold, his train coming around the corner, the rails and the electric wires turning into lines of light, closer and closer, and then this blinding light, like if the moon were as bright as the sun, and he walked out of it. He

had a big down coat, it squished when I hugged him.
That's about it.

PHIL: You had a whole marriage before you were the
age I am now.

GRACE: Phil. I have never been the age you are now.

PHIL: Maybe you were and you don't remember.

GRACE: Yeah. I'd hate to see that happen to...someone I
cared about. *(Pause)* Pull over?

PHIL: Why?

GRACE: You heard me.

(The motor stops. Crickets. Starlight)

PHIL: Now what?

(GRACE kisses PHIL hungrily.)

PHIL: Umph!

(GRACE's hands are all over PHIL and he responds in kind.)

PHIL: Wow. Watch out for the— *(The horn honks.)* We
could move to the back, if you—

*(The horn honks. And again. And again, in a faster and
faster rhythm. The horn sound holds, and fades.)*

Scene Four

*(Darkness, lights, engine, wind. PHIL is driving. He is
nodding a little. On the passenger side, GRACE opens her
eyes and stretches.)*

GRACE: Hi.

PHIL: Hi.

GRACE: Where are we?

PHIL: I don't know.

GRACE: What time is it?

PHIL: I bet this is a dumb question. Right in front of us, is there a gigantic black bat guiding us down the road?

(GRACE *looks. Pause*)

GRACE: Yes there is.

PHIL: Thought so. The tips of its wings are touching the wheels?

GRACE: Yup. Gliding.

PHIL: The moon's behind us. It's the shadow of the car.

GRACE: Looks more like a bat.

(He is shaking his head to stay awake.)

GRACE: Think we need to rest?

PHIL: I'm okay.

(Pause)

GRACE: That was something back there.

PHIL: It was great.

GRACE: Yes it was. Listen. If I tell you something, will you try to remember it later?

PHIL: Sure.

GRACE: You are the most wonderful lover.

PHIL: You are, too.

GRACE: Just—remember I said so. *(Pause)* I have to tell you something.

PHIL: Great.

GRACE: No. Once we get home. I think it would be better if you didn't see me anymore.

PHIL: What?

GRACE: I could have waited till we got back, I mean I know this is going to make the rest of the drive kind of long, or we could have gotten back and I'd start waiting longer and longer to return your phone calls and see if it sort of dried up on its own. But I didn't, because I want to make sure that you know that this isn't about you. You are a treasure. Okay? It's me. I can't—you love to do so many things, but I have to start thinking about—other things—that—

PHIL: Like what? What things?

GRACE: I don't know!

PHIL: You do. You won't tell me.

GRACE: I know you. It would be so easy for me—God! —To hear you make a lot of promises right now. But I can't.

PHIL: I did something. I went wrong somewhere.

GRACE: No.

PHIL: I must have. It's because I'm younger than you.

GRACE: Phil, I just—I couldn't bear to go through life being the person who always tells you "No."

PHIL: This is not what—I drove all this way—

GRACE: We'd better go home.

PHIL: No.

GRACE: I knew I couldn't do this without hurting somebody, and now I have, so let's just go home, okay?

PHIL: No.

GRACE: What do you mean, "No"?

PHIL: I can't.

GRACE: Why not?

PHIL: I'm scared.

GRACE: Don't be scared.

PHIL: If I drive home I don't see you again.

GRACE: Phil.

PHIL: So I don't want to go home anymore.

GRACE: I *have* to say this, I don't want to, but—I have to get back in time for work. Okay?

PHIL: Maybe. I don't know. Maybe we're blowing off work today.

GRACE: I can't do that.

PHIL: I'm never going to see you again and you want to go to work?

GRACE: It's necessary.

PHIL: It's money. This is love. Listen.

GRACE: Sweet baby, this isn't a credit card commercial. This is me needing to keep my medical insurance. The rules of life don't screech to a halt because we love each other.

PHIL: They should.

GRACE: Yes. They should. But they won't. And I *can't*... Having to tell you stuff like this is going to break my heart.

PHIL: I love you.

GRACE: I love you, too. Now drive me home.

(PHIL *shakes his head.*)

GRACE: Phil. You want to drive away from your responsibilities. That's great, you do that. But I cannot come along.

(PHIL *looks at* GRACE.)

GRACE: Watch the road.

(PHIL *keeps looking at* GRACE.)

PHIL: If you were a thousand miles away and my credit was gone and my money was gone and I couldn't rent a car or take a bus or hitchhike or borrow a car because I had no job and my friends would all have forgotten my name, I would walk all the way to you in my shoes and if I didn't have my shoes then I would walk it barefoot, because *that* I think is my responsibility.

(PHIL *turns toward the road. Pause.*)

GRACE: You've been driving all night, haven't you?

PHIL: We needed to get away.

GRACE: We can't keep going like this forever. Eventually we're going to reach the ocean.

PHIL: We can sit on the beach. I'll watch you get a tan.

(*Snow begins to fall.*)

GRACE: Too much sun is bad for you.

PHIL: I'll buy you a hat.

GRACE: Uh, Phil?

PHIL: Hm.

GRACE: Is that snow? Phil, I see snow falling on the car.

PHIL: Probably very light hail.

(GRACE *sticks an arm out the window.*)

GRACE: Not cold...

PHIL: Some kind of pollen?

(PHIL *is nodding again.*)

GRACE: (*Wicked Witch of the East voice*) Poppies... poppies...

(PHIL *opens his eyes with a jolt.*)

PHIL: Woof! Man!

GRACE: You okay?

PHIL: I had this dream.

GRACE: When?

PHIL: Just now.

GRACE: Pull over, Phil.

PHIL: I dreamt I was driving a car—

GRACE: Which is what you are doing, keep it in mind.

(GRACE *turns on the radio. Static, then, a big band dance tune. The lights change to the dance floor.* PHIL *opens the car door and starts to get out. She yanks him back.*)

GRACE: Phil! What the hell are you doing!

PHIL: I—what?

GRACE: Stay in the car!

PHIL: Wo.

GRACE: What were you doing?

PHIL: I thought I was having another flashback.

GRACE: Phil, how's about I do some driving, huh?

PHIL: I'm okay now. Really. Got my second wind.

(*Blackout. Crazy headlights. A long screech. A metallic crunch.*)

Scene Five

(GRACE *is sitting on the ground near the car.* PHIL *is standing over her. Light from a streetlight through a chainlink fence.*)

GRACE: I'm fine.

PHIL: Stay sitting. You may be in shock.

GRACE: I swear to you I am absolutely fine.

PHIL: Lucky we didn't roll it.

GRACE: Are you okay?

PHIL: Couple of scratches getting out. No problem. I wonder where we are.

GRACE: Is there a sign?

PHIL: I'll go look. Something's got to say.

(PHIL *crosses away and peers into the darkness.* GRACE *furtively checks herself for blood. He comes back into the light.*)

GRACE: So where'd we land?

PHIL: Louisville.

GRACE: Kentucky?

PHIL: I don't know. Probably a lot of Louisvilles around.

GRACE: If it's Kentucky, you know what that means?

PHIL: Home of the Louisville Slugger.

GRACE: Finest wood ever to strike a baseball. Wow. You did it. Excellent destination. Oh, my God.

PHIL: What?

GRACE: Before we crashed. You said the car was being guided.

PHIL: Right. Big flapping bat.

GRACE: Phil! A *bat* guided us to *Louisville.* You see? Granted, I mean, one is an animal and one is sporting equipment, but the *word*—

PHIL: Grace. I may have put too much emphasis on this omen thing.

GRACE: But you see?

PHIL: We had an accident, that's all.

GRACE: We had an accident. An accident. Oh, God.

PHIL: What?

GRACE: You're right, I was wrong about the bat stuff. It's this. We've had an accident. Oh, Phil. Oh, jeez.

(PHIL *holds* GRACE *and rocks her on the ground.*)

PHIL: I know. It's okay. We've had a little accident. I know.

(Grace looks at Phil.)

GRACE: You do know.

PHIL: Well, jeez, Grace, I drive a thousand miles waiting for you to tell me something. There's not a lot of things it's gonna be.

GRACE: Give the boy a cigar.

PHIL: What, uh... What confused me, see, was that you'd said you weren't pregnant.

GRACE: I guess I did that, yeah.

PHIL: I kept waiting for you to tell me. I kept trying to help you tell me.

GRACE: Yeah. I figured that out.

PHIL: You could see what I was doing. And you still couldn't tell me. My whole life, I say, "You know what's great? You know what I love?" Anything I can think of to say, everybody knows it. So I'm this idiot.

GRACE: No, Phil—

PHIL: First time you talked I said, "Finally. Finally. Someone who will tell me anything." The good, the bad, if it's true I want it. My whole life. This shit. *(He turns away and cries.)*

GRACE: Phil. Poor sweet boy.

(Phil turns on Grace.)

PHIL: *Stop.* Calling me that. *(Pause)* How long.

GRACE: About four weeks.

PHIL: Four—

GRACE: Two weeks I didn't know. One week I wasn't sure. One week I was too scared to know. Phil, I was so scared I didn't even want to take the test. I took it today.

PHIL: A *month* you've been thinking about it. Never a word. That *shit* about Suzannah being pregnant. What was that?

GRACE: A trial balloon? I was looking for a way to—

PHIL: A month. Now I'm gonna think about everything that happened this month.

GRACE: Hey. You really wanted to help me out, why didn't you call me on it? Huh? Do you know what I've been going through?

PHIL: No. You didn't tell me.

GRACE: Because I was scared to death of what you'd do if you knew.

PHIL: Is it somebody else's?

GRACE: What?

PHIL: Is it?

GRACE: Who else's could it be?

PHIL: I don't know. I guess I don't know much.

GRACE: Are you accusing me of seeing someone else?

PHIL: You've been hiding one important thing, maybe you're hiding another one.

GRACE: What do you think I am?

PHIL: You're a liar.

GRACE: I didn't lie, I concealed something I didn't think you were ready to hear. Sometimes you have to do that when you're talking to a child.

PHIL: Cut it out!

GRACE: Why should I have told you? What good was it going to do me? I'm trying to figure out whether to change my whole life around and you're going, "Mo-om, Grace gots my baby and she won't share it with me! It's not fai-air!"

PHIL: You really are a bitch, Grace.

GRACE: Finally figured that out, huh?

PHIL: I was right. It is somebody else's child. Is that
what you want? Fine. It's one hundred percent your
child. God help it.

GRACE: You—

PHIL: Someone gives you his heart, you treat him like
he's holding a piece of shit! You'll make a *great* mother,
yeah!

GRACE: Never. *Ever.* Tell me I shouldn't be a mother.
You of *all* people! How dare you tell me a child of mine
needs God's help or anybody's help? What do you
think a mother is, Phil, a nice warm lap? It's shitloads
of stamina and blood in your eye and anything else it
needs, you've got to be there and be there and be there.
It's not fun. It's not a romance. It's love. I've waited
half my life to do this and I put it off and put it off
waiting till I turned into warm and fuzzy Mamma, well
fuck that and fuck you, if I want a baby I'll have a baby
and *raise* it and anybody tries to come between us, oh,
God help 'em!

(GRACE *and* PHIL *stand there and stare at each other, too
afraid to move. Long pause*)

PHIL: I bet the car still runs.

GRACE: What? I didn't—

PHIL: The car. It should get us back.

GRACE: Give me the keys.

PHIL: No, I can—

GRACE: Get some sleep.

(PHIL *takes the keys from his pocket and crosses to hand
them to her. They trudge to the car and get in.* GRACE *starts
the car and drives. Long pause*)

PHIL: Listen. Whatever you decide. Would it help if we moved in together?

GRACE: What?

PHIL: I've been running some figures in my head, kind of a rough budget, and I think we could save maybe twenty percent off our combined expenses now. We could get a bigger place for less than we pay for two little ones, plus phone, plus utilities, and then food, big saving there, plus we could commute together, save on gas, parking—

GRACE: Commute together.

PHIL: Yeah. Couldn't we?

GRACE: To work.

PHIL: Oh. Well, yeah. My company doesn't have parental leave. We should, but we don't. *(He yawns deeply.)* I ought to talk to Jack my boss about that.

GRACE: Get some sleep.

PHIL: Think about it though?

(GRACE nods. PHIL climbs into the back seat and curls up. Engine. Lights. Howling wind. She adjusts the rear view mirror and looks back at him. Softly, a baby begins to cry. She listens. He sits up sleepily and kisses her on the cheek.)

PHIL: It's okay, I'll go.

(GRACE watches PHIL leave the car and cross downstage. He has a baseball glove on one hand, with a baseball in the pocket.)

PHIL: Hey. Hey, pal. *(He kneels and speaks at baby height.)* Look—buddy, look at this. This is a baseball glove. It goes on your hand. *(He holds it out.)* You wear it to catch a baseball. *(He drops the baseball out of the pocket into his other hand.)* Pal. This is a baseball. A special baseball. *(He holds the ball and turns it over.)* You see this mark? Dan Gladden left that mark when he hit this

ball with a baseball bat. He hit it so hard that it flew all
the way up to a box in the sky where your Mom and I
were watching. You see this here? He signed this ball.
See? Dan. Gladden. This is for you, pal. *(He puts the ball
back in the glove.)* These are yours.

*(GRACE watches PHIL as he waits and listens until the
sobbing fades away. Lights down on him.)*

*(GRACE begins picking up speed. She smiles. The car is
going faster and faster as the lights fade.)*

Scene Six

*(The car, in noonday sunlight. No one visible. Then PHIL's
arms stretch luxuriantly up from the passenger side.)*

PHIL: Mmmm. *(Pause. He sits bolt upright, feeling
frantically in front of him with his hands.)* Mngah! *(His left
hand finds the steering wheel, to his left. He looks. He is not
driving.)* Grace? *(She's not in the car. He opens the door
and puts out a tentative toe. Yes, the car is really stopped.
He gets out of the car and looks around.)* Grace? *(He looks
around, baffled.)* Where the hell am I?

*(GRACE enters, still wearing her road clothes, thoroughly
dazed. She carries a cassette tape. PHIL looks up and sees
her.)*

PHIL: Where'd you go?

GRACE: Didn't want to wake you... *(She leans on the hood
of the car.)*

PHIL: What time is it?

GRACE: I don't know...

PHIL: Where are we?

GRACE: I'm going to say something...

PHIL: I'm not very awake here.

GRACE: I'm gonna have the baby.

(PHIL *stands up fast.*)

GRACE: Quick! What are you thinking!

PHIL: Uh.

GRACE: Right now! Don't sugarcoat it!

PHIL: Rookie from the country!

GRACE: What?

PHIL: Rookie from the country. Grace, you're gonna—

GRACE: What rookie from the country?

PHIL: All of them, you know.

GRACE: No, I don't.

PHIL: Old-time ballplayer story—boy's never seen the city, big club calls him up, you know, that one.

GRACE: This is what you're thinking.

PHIL: Very first picture, swear to God. The rookie tells a cab driver to take him to the ballpark, and they pull up outside the biggest damn building he's ever seen. He walks inside the walls. And far away, he sees a diamond. The team is taking batting practice, the rookie can see stars he's only dreamed about, hearing games late at night on the radio. He starts to walk toward them, to tell them he's here, he's finally here.

GRACE: And a guard walks up to throw him out.

PHIL: Yes! Always!

GRACE: And the guard says, "What do you think you're doing?"

PHIL: And the rookie says, "This is where I'm gonna play ball."

GRACE: And the guard says, "I bet you think you're pretty good."

PHIL: And the rookie looks at his team. And he says, "Yeah."

(Pause)

GRACE: I *love* that story. That is *great.*

PHIL: Can I tell you something? I've never told this to anyone.

GRACE: Go ahead.

PHIL: Lots of times... Lots of times I don't even *like* baseball.

GRACE: What?

PHIL: Come on, admit it, the game is slow. Nothing much happens. By July the season feels like it'll never get done, and they're still only halfway home. Look, when I was five years old the Twins won the division. Got swept by the Orioles in the playoffs. Broke my heart. The next year they finished twenty-six and a half games out of first. But every night I listened to the games. Every morning I read the box scores. I never stopped going to the park. In '87 they were the World Champions. Last year they were dead last. I never stopped rooting.

GRACE: What are you trying to say?

PHIL: Grace, I'm a baseball fan. I know how to make a commitment.

GRACE: Phil. It's only a game.

PHIL: Right. It's only a *game.* And I've been following that every day for twenty-one years. You would be my *family.*

(GRACE's face crumples a bit.)

PHIL: You're crying.

GRACE: It's okay, Phil. It's a good cry. Does your tape player work?

PHIL: Yeah. There's a thing you have to do with a screwdriver.

(GRACE *holds out the cassette.*)

GRACE: Come on.

(GRACE *and* PHIL *get in the car, her in the driver's seat. She puts the tape in the tape deck. He monkeys with it.*)

PHIL: So where are we?

GRACE: I found a clinic.

PHIL: Are you okay?

GRACE: They have this Mister Microphone thing they put against your tummy.

(*A deep and rhythmic pounding, and another, softer and faster sound. It's the beat from the beginning of the first and second acts.*)

PHIL: What is that?

GRACE: Heartbeats. Mine's the loud one.

PHIL: Wow.

(GRACE *and* PHIL *listen for a while.*)

PHIL: So where are we going?

GRACE: Well. Kids gonna take a little trip.

PHIL: I am?

GRACE: We are. Want to come?

(PHIL *nods vigorously. The engine roars, and the heartbeats fade into it.*)

PHIL: So where're those Kids headed, Vin?

GRACE: Down the Mississippi, Red. The report is they're driving so fast the radar can't pick 'em up. Aaaand it looks like they're headed for Texas.

PHIL: Vin, it looks like they're California bound!

GRACE: They're headed for the beach. Red, they've got surfboards!

PHIL: They're paddling west!

GRACE: Kids' gonna see the world!

PHIL: There is nothing this Kid cannot do!

GRACE: Kid's landed in Asia and hit the ground running.

PHIL: Freeing Tibet singlehanded, Vin!

GRACE: The Kid cannot stop, just cannot stop!

PHIL: Finding everyone a homeland!

GRACE: Helping Europe make decent popular music!

PHIL: Vin, the Kid is raising the Titanic!

GRACE: Raising Babe Ruth from the dead—

PHIL: And trading him back to Boston!

GRACE: This Kid is *great*!

PHIL: Making Detroit build a really great roadster again!

GRACE: I *love* this Kid!

PHIL: The Kid is climbing into that car!

GRACE: He's turning on the radio!

PHIL: The World Series is on!

GRACE: And the Kid is at the plate!

PHIL: Here comes the pitch—

GRACE: The bases are loaded for the Kid—

PHIL: He swings!

GRACE: It's a towering drive!

PHIL: Lou Gehrig is running!

GRACE: Cool Papa Bell is running!

PHIL: Roberto Clemente is flying!

GRACE: The ball clears the fence!

PHIL: The ball leaves the park!

GRACE: As it goes out of sight it is rising...

PHIL: The Kid rounds the bases and heads for home...

GRACE: And the Kid...

PHIL: The Kid has a heartbeat.

(PHIL *holds up one hand.* GRACE *slaps her own into it. They clasp hands.*)

PHIL: Jeez, I love you.

GRACE: I love you so much.

(GRACE *and* PHIL *kiss.*)

GRACE: Phil.

(*The kiss goes on.*)

GRACE: Phil, there's something else.

PHIL: Something *else*?

GRACE: When the doctor listened to the microphone thing she heard something funny and she did a test to be sure.

PHIL: Oh my God. Is it healthy? Is it all right?

GRACE: They're fine.

PHIL: They're—

(*Pause*)

GRACE: It's twins.

PHIL: You're kidding. It's twins?

GRACE: We got a bonus baby.

PHIL: It's TWINS?

GRACE: It's an omen.

PHIL: Wow. Hey, you know what's great?

GRACE: Yeah.

(GRACE *and* PHIL *smile at each other. Heartbeats and music.*
The lights fade.)

END OF PLAY

www.ingramcontent.com/pod-product-compliance
Lightning Source LLC
Chambersburg PA
CBHW052213090426
42741CB00010B/2526